WILD HONEY, TOUGH SALT

WILD HONEY, TOUGH SALT

poems

Kim Stafford

Red Hen Press | *Pasadena, CA*

Wild Honey, Tough Salt
Copyright © 2019 by Kim Stafford

Book design by Mark E. Cull

Library of Congress Cataloging-in-Publication Data

Names: Stafford, Kim Robert, author.
Title: Wild honey, tough salt : poems / Kim Stafford.
Description: First edition. | Pasadena, CA : Red Hen Press, [2019]
Identifiers: LCCN 2018056200 | ISBN 9781597098960 (tradepaper)
Classification: LCC PS3569.T23 W55 2019 | DDC 811/.54—dc23
LC record available at https://lccn.loc.gov/2018056200

The National Endowment for the Arts, the Los Angeles County Arts Commission, the Ahmanson Foundation, the Dwight Stuart Youth Fund, the Max Factor Family Foundation, the Pasadena Tournament of Roses Foundation, the Pasadena Arts & Culture Commission and the City of Pasadena Cultural Affairs Division, the City of Los Angeles Department of Cultural Affairs, the Audrey & Sydney Irmas Charitable Foundation, the Kinder Morgan Foundation, the Allergan Foundation, and the Riordan Foundation partially support Red Hen Press.

First Edition
Published by Red Hen Press
www.redhen.org

Acknowledgments

Thanks to the editors of the following publications for their kind hospitality:

Some of these poems first appeared in *Café Review, Camas Magazine, Cirque, Cloudbank, Friends of William Stafford Newsletter, The Grove Review, High Desert Journal, Image, ISLE, Jefferson Monthly, LC Review, Miramar, Mountain Gazette, Open Spaces, Oregon English Journal, Oregon Historical Quarterly, The Oregonian, Orion, Pangyrus, Plainsongs, Poetry Northwest, Portland Magazine, Salamander, The Shop* (Ireland), *The Sun, The Texas Observer, Timberline Review,* and *Windfall*.

"A Buddhist in Cattle Country" first appeared in *Home Land: Ranching and a West That Works,* ed. Laura Pritchett, Richard Knight, and Jeff Lee (Boulder, CO: Johnson Books, 2007).

"At the Indian Cemetery, Oregon Coast" first appeared in *Poets of the American West,* ed. Lowell Jaeger (Kalispell, MT: Many Voices Press, 2010).

"Aunt Mar Changes How We See" first appeared on the website *150 Kansas Poems*.

"Champion the Enemy's Need" and an earlier version of "Citizen of Dark Times" first appeared in *The Flavor of Unity,* a chapbook (Portland, OR: Little Infinities, 2017).

"Earth Verse" was composed as an element for a public art project in Oregon City, OR, where the poem is etched into stainless steel as part of "Perennial," an installation by Aaron Hussey. "Abe & I," "Earth Verse," "In My Name," "Palouse," and "What Civilization Costs" first appeared in *Earth Verse,* a chapbook (Portland, OR: Little Infinities, 2017).

"Prairie Prescription" and "Willa Cather's Ride" first appeared in *Prairie Prescription,* a chapbook (Limberlost Press, 2011), and "How to Sleep Cold," "My Iron Catastrophe," "Notes from the Storm," and "Once in the Back Country" first appeared in *How to Sleep Cold,* a chapbook (Boise, ID: Limberlost Press, 2018).

"Love Money" appeared on the website of PBS NewsHour.

"Mediation" first appeared in *Poetry Speaks Who I Am: Poems of Discovery, Inspiration, Independence, and Everything Else,* ed. Elise Paschen (Naperville, IL: Sourcebooks, 2010).

"Nado, the Good Guardian" first appeared in *Legacy of Beginning: Poems in Bhutan*, a limited-edition book from Larkspur Press in 2013.

"Proclamation for Peace" first appeared (as "Friend: Download This Free Proclamation") as a limited-edition broadside (Eugene: Knight Library Press), as did "Lucky 4 a.m." (Portland: Pacific NW College of Art), and "A Prayer by the Tigris" (Eugene, OR: lone goose press).

"The Right to Be Forgotten," "Peace Warrior," "A Few Treasured Steps at Glensallagh," and "Roe Deer" first appeared in *The Right to Be Forgotten*, a chapbook (Portland, OR: Little Infinities, 2017).

Note: "It Seemed Like an Ordinary Day Until I Had Coffee With Jesus at the Café du Monde" is the title of a painting by Bill Hemmerling at the Café du Monde in New Orleans, LA.

Thanks to the Sitka Center for Art & Ecology on the Oregon coast for retreat time to complete this book. Thanks to Bill Howe and Joy Bottinelli for their support of my work. And thanks to my wife Perrin for her sustaining belief in my creations.

CONTENTS

1
ECONOMY OF MIRACLES

2
THE TORTURER'S WIFE

3

LOST LEAVES OF EARTH

4
Marriage in Dog Years

1

Economy of Miracles

How to Sleep Cold in North County

You didn't bring the bedding that you need.
Last night's thunder cleared the sky.
Tonight, the stars could cut your tent's
thin skin to tatters, and the moon
bullies up through the pines. Out beyond
the meadow, elk whistle and stamp.
You settle in, wearing all you've got.
It's not a sleeping bag tonight,
but a thin cocoon for metamorphosis.
Make a snout, a breathing hole,
and burrow in, writhing to survive.
In darkness, cold is the blunt force
stretching time to an elastic misery
that gathers all you ever did wrong,
that tunnels through your geologic story—
you a yeasty bit in the great extinction.

Then morning comes. A sleepy robin
ladles out forgiveness. Light seeps in.
Rise, poor pilgrim, and bless the sun.

The Secret

After long delay, ignorant of what you guarded
before it came volcanic to your mind, there to be
hoarded smoldering until you found a way to tell it,
your secret is out—your joy too tender to entrust
to anyone, your pain too dangerous to reveal
until you do. And there it is, a birth, with blood,
to celebrate.
        Then the bowl in the heart,
where such things first appear, has something
new to hide, some fingerling creature silver
in the dark, with jagged fins and tender wings
that must be gripped, locked up, suppressed, fed
crumbs as you fend off the world. *Little one,*
must you leave me now?

Thus we breathe our secrets one by one.

Benign Indignities

I have walked a thousand times
this mile at Port Townsend to witness
how waves churn, thrash, and ebb.
And I have lifted stones once shattered
from bedrock in the deep, but then
made shapely by water's way
with time and change. I have learned
from that tug and surrender how to
fondle what is jagged until it is smooth.

So in the book of my humiliations
I am taught to cherish my myriad failures
now rounded by recollection, thorns caressed
until they shine, secret stupidities pearled
by affection. I have kept no dignity—only
saved this wild museum of errors where I walk
along the sea, marveling at what I have survived.

My Iron Catastrophe

Everything was going to hell. In a few years
my marriage ended, my brother took his life, my father
fell down dead in the kitchen, and by some elastic anomaly

nights grew longer, darker, and days grew gray, food
tasted of sawdust, music withered, the sun was blunted
by some bitter pall. Words failed. Feet grew heavy.

"Is this growing old?"

Then a friend demanded—on a trail into the wilderness—
"What do you want, Kim Stafford?" "I want to be
a good father." "No," said the friend, "not about

your daughter—you." "I want to be a good writer, then."
"Not about words. You." I thought and thought. Sun
spun a filament of web from one hemlock to another,

and as the strand bellied and swayed, an iridescence
swam from one end to the other. "I want to be honest,"
I said. "In parenting, writing, friendship, witness on earth,

I want to be honest." "Yes," said the friend. "You have
not chosen an easy thing, but you have chosen."
In that moment, the catastrophe began to end,

and the hard centering to begin.

Love Money

I heard it on the news: most charity
is sent by poor people to poorer people—
five, six, eight hundred billion across borders
each year: a father sweeping in London
for his family in Bangalore, a mother changing
sheets in Dubai for her children in Kathmandu,
a brother weeding lettuce in the San Joaquin
to fund his younger brother's dream in Michoacán.

For without the younger brother's dream
this would be too hard a life. Without
the children there, the bent back here would
hurt with no remedy. Without the broom
at Trafalgar Square restoring clean stone,
there would be no way to love at this
distance, no long-flying bird to send
a song for the little ones growing taller

with only a smudged photo of their
patron ghost, with that crooked smile.

Tove Jansson's Island

Her father sculpted in bronze
and her mother designed postage stamps—
great forms and fine detail her first food.
Little hands silently lifting a mallet
or burin, getting the heft of creation.

Sun and pollen, ruby ants in a row—
her ears filled with the breath of waves,
her schooling a blur of breathless pleasures
far from anything countable. (What boy
could match a bird's fine wit?)

When she was grown, a boat
would take her to the island without
landing, and she would leap into the sea
to guide the crate of a summer's simple
food to shore, as the boat circled away.

No clock or voice, no growl of motor
or purr of phone, she would delve
into the bounty of her young silence
to hum songs she smuggled into wind,
as dozing became dreams, dreams stories

old and odd and native, bristling
with thought more like pine cones
or glittering seams in bedrock
than anything anyone had ever
known—stories of summer light,

of star seeds concentric around hints,
stones held like sorrows, leaves watched
unfurling hour by hour, lit feather lifting away
across the sea in the general drift
of hidden happiness.

When autumn came, the boat brought exile.
She wintered on gritty streets by the gong
of streetcar clang, wires across the sky,
the naked glory of creation dressed
in small decisions, minor laws—until

summer, summer, summer . . . story,
story, story . . . then night and morning,
word and silence. Old, she finished—hut
empty, pages topped by a stone the sea
had shaped with its scarf of centuries.

WHAT CIVILIZATION COSTS

When moon comes up, and we sleep
outside, just there in the aspen grove, a lone
coyote cuts loose with abandon banging
all the silver pans of its voice, raveling

a spiral cry up like smoke
at the moon's command. Shiver all
you want, tame human—feel the pang
of what it must be to sing like that,

to squander your whole life
in a single breath, again and
again from growl to soprano
for one long glissando toward stars.

We pay dearly for all we have given up.
In the morning, instead of biting song,
like pilgrims we go down there, bent low,
seeking a print in the dust.

Willa Cather's Ride

They say, at ten, Willa rode her pony from Red Cloud
out to immigrant farms to deliver mail, scuffed letters
from the old country, exotically stamped, slit open
by homesteader's trembling hands, and then came tears.

They say, out of her girl heart's mercy, she knew then
she must read the letters first, and so prepare a remedy
before delivery—a story to tell, an antidote to hard news,
a way to open country people before their sorrows came.

This is how, they say, little Willa became a writer, one who
carries what she knows before others across the prairie
from town to the lonesome soddy where only a girl's
bright eyes can save an old woman's strange love forever.

Professor's House, Death Comes, One of Ours, Ántonia
all began with a wild canter across that open ground
on a mission of mercy, Willa's hair flying in the wind
and a story gathering in her mind like a storm.

PRAIRIE PRESCRIPTION

"You have been weakened," the doctor said, "by your first two
children's births. This time you must obey without fail or you will die.
Harrison, are you hearing this? I prescribe an hour of beauty a day."

Back at the farm, at evening, Lottie retired to the rocker on the porch
while the fields turned velvet with purple and gold. Crickets tuned
their little drums, and the breeze brought pollen from paradise.

The dishtowel on its hook, laundry basket tipped at the wall,
socks not darned, bread not baked, the quilt pieced in its box
unsewn. Lottie folded her hands and gazed far into the shadows.

Each day, an hour of pure sky poured into the child curled
inside her, slanted sunlight braided into the rising, looming moon
she tasted and swallowed, a thimble of starlight, a sip of dew.

When the night came at last—the harrowing umbilical tangle
inside her—the doctor sent Harrison and the children to the barn to pray,
while inside Lottie all that light and color and music and holy stillness

clenched, writhed, and with a wild song my mother was born.

Nado: the Good Guardian
at Ogyen Choling in Bhutan

Who are we to say, when Nado begins to bark
in the night outside our sleeping place, he has not
protected us from a fierce ghost come to take a soul?

Or perhaps the leopard has come along the thorny
margin of the field to take another of our young foals.
The dog delivers thirty-two barks, like hard, round beads,

and the ghost thinks twice, the leopard turns, uncertain,
Who are we to say this good guardian, with frost
on the fur of his back, was not one of us in another life,

and now comes home to protect his people?
Twenty-eight insistent barks, then a breath. Fourteen
barks. Then a round of four-bark bursts:

    om mani peme hum.

After all, he must face himself in the dusky mirror
of a frozen puddle when dawn comes. So now,
in the deep dark, while the foal trembles in the stall,

the leopard crouches among thorns, the restless ghost
turns at the window, and we human listeners
hold this waking vigil, hour by hour, our good
guardian keeps on chanting honestly for our protection.
Who are we, in our safe beds, to say he is not
the turning between the living and the lost?

Who are we?

Notes from the Storm at Billy Meadow

In the night, lightning x-rayed my tent and the torrent
found passage from faulty seam to everything dry to me,
and I remembered Thunder-Rolling-in-the-Mountains when
the bolt flashed, rain nails drove down, and I had to be
lost along the dark forest road in wet skin and flailing coat,
to be lit by fire, then blind on earth, walking
toward a meeting with my real name.

There was no way in that dark when wild fury came to
find me I could not be walking the luminous road hammered
by rain so fierce it stung. There was no way safety, comfort,
or good sense could prevail over the wild child spirit
that yet ruled my body staggering the fiery rut.

At the end, when this storm of days is done,
when calm glides toward my eyes, remind me:
"Beyond that dark door is who you are."

Once in the Back Country

At the rim I left the road and went down
lost along path of elk and deer, staggered
into folded clefts, slid into ravines, stepped
bald ridges, tumbled scree, skirted cliffs
past the choke point, drifted over the saddle
and down through stands of young pine at the burn
until they opened to sun-thick lupine and crimson
paintbrush, salsify, mullein, ragged lilac
by the stony field where failed
homesteaders left their rusted
hay knife thrust in earth, hickory
handles bleached white where the man's
hands let go, where Joseph Creek
ran fast below the sagging shack twitching
with curtain shreds and yawning roof
and beyond it all, the cave they lived in
first, when the cabin was a rising box
of sap-gold pine poles at dawn, then
retreated to at last with bedspring, dishpan,
ax and two-handed plow asleep
on its side—the place they maybe said
"We'll come back someday. Don't
cry. You'll see . . ." and there, just inside
the cave's drip-line, three pair of boots
curled and cracked: heavy man's
thick soles, slender woman's
lace-ups, and the child's pried
open one last time and left there
where they stepped back barefoot into Eden.

Weaving Kin

Sometimes a Bella Coola woman needs a Bella Coola man
to leave the coast, step upriver, thread the small streams
through forest, and climb into the bare crags to find
the lightning-shattered stump of the whitebark pine
close against the cliff where mountain goats as they
shouldered through the slot left slubs, tangled gobs,
and long strands of white wool—the man to wander,
hunger, seek and find enough to fill a seal-skin bag—
and then to turn, in the trance of his quest go down
from the crags, stumble through thickets of salmonberry,
follow the small streams through forest and meadow,
and then the river to the sea.

Then the Bella Coola man needs the Bella Coola woman
to take her spindle stick long as her arm, belted with a whorl
of alder wood carved with two salmon swimming round
and against the flat of her thigh to spin the shredded
inner bark of cedar wrapped with wool until she has
enough, ball by ball and skein by skein to dye black
with root of fern, and yellow with ripened urine, and
pale blue with a secret of her own, and then suspend
her yarn over a horizontal pole, each strand weighted
with sea stones knocking softly one to another
as she begins to weave her kin lineage: square ears
of bear, spread wings of raven, eye of eagle, fin of whale

until the blanket is broad enough to cover her shoulders
and abalone at her ears, her eyes flashing in shadow
where the man can see her across the firelight
at the winter ceremonial as they listen to the old stories
that weave together whale, sea, salmon, river, the small
streams, forest, mountain, thunder, all kin joined so that
when the time is right, cedar smoke and fur, starlight
through the smoke hole, all food gathered and stored
in bentwood box and sealskin pouch, nettle net folded,
sinew rope coiled—then the fingers of the man may
comb the long dark hair of the woman, and the fingers
of the woman the long dark hair of the man.

Mediation

At the dinner table, before the thrown
plate, but after the bitter claim,
in that one beat of silence
before the parents declare war

their child, who until now had been
invisible, but who had learned in school
a catechism, speaks: "Would you like me
to help solve the conflict?" Silence.

They can't look at each other. A glance
would sear the soul. A wall of fire plots
this Maginot line across the butter plate
splits salt from pepper, him from her.

So their child speaks: "Three rules, then:
One—you have to let each other finish.
Two—you have to tell the truth. Three—
you have to *want* to solve the conflict.

If you say yes, we will solve it.
I love you. What do you say?"

My Critics Have Erred

In their assessment of my résumé
they have it mostly right, if only
outcomes were the thing—paltry

and peripheral. Compare intentions
to completion? One drop of rain
to the ocean's plan. I did not

stop the war, even the war
in me. Fitful fighting smolders
in the provinces, while the capitol

remains under siege after all
these years of strife. But they
forgot: I still remember

that canary in the redbud tree.

Wild Honey, Tough Salt

Why do these things come touch my sleeve—
a dream of my father working the fields, a bird
singing before first light, a sense in my body that now
I can do the hard things? I stay in place and changes
come. I do not move and I am moved, crowded
by legions of crisis and sweetness.

Salt and honey—harder to tell the difference now.

A friend does beauty without cause, it is honey.
A friend dies after pure pain, we feel an odd
sweetness knowing with a jolt her pure passage—
like the time those monks gave up their old vat of wine,
poured it out down the road, a sudden purple scarf
along the stones alive with bees and butterflies

gone crazy with sweetness as it passed away.

It Seemed Like an Ordinary Day until
I Had Coffee with Jesus at the Café du Monde

I didn't know shattered curb could pillow his head until
a black man sleeping on Barracks showed me at dawn.
I didn't know the brick shop-corner on Decatur could brace

a woman's back while her lover softly mauled her, brushed
her face. They taught me. I didn't know the Tarot Reader
must have eyes that tunnel sorrow and the light beyond

at Jackson Square, where a shawled man, setting his
flimsy table, revealed to me. I didn't know a smudge
of woman could yet be standing in turquoise socks—

not begging, not speaking, not looking away—trembling
vigil where I passed her yesterday. She made me see. Didn't
know invisible inside the steel kitchen at Café du Monde

a voice could sing against the hiss and clang her
stubborn, human thrill. Who taught her that?
I didn't know a man so strung out he could

barely stand would roll under a moving train, lie still
on ties and ballast while the wheels sliced past,
then roll over the second rail and stagger to his feet.

I thought I would see him die, thought I would be
called to hear his last curse. I didn't know a woman
bespeckled like secretary in pink flimsy stuff could be

so stoned she'd pause to shimmer, totter, tremble, and
drill my gaze before moving on. Now I know. What do I know?
I didn't know the singer at the Spotted Cat so deep

inside music so loud her words could not prevail—dueling
trumpets, trombone, guitar, bass, and Washboard Chaz—
could yet transcend the room dense with dancers an ache

that stung my hands and feet. I didn't know JT the bartender
at Flanagan's, after Katrina, named his souped-up Lincoln
Rocinante to reach top speed at Bonneville, but when Hillary

appeared on the big screen to concede, turned off the juke
to hear her every word. *She did well.* I didn't know a man could
curl asleep on Decatur with a baby-cradled gas stove in his arms.

If these pilgrims be ordinary, they raise me, take in, turn me over
inside out. I didn't know I could see the human ravel to a thread,
then be knit precarious. I didn't know I would rather be mule,

moon over Algiers, skittish ferry spun on the river's brawn, human
wreckage on a bench who bleats, *How ya doin'? Spare change?*
I didn't know the pigeon flattened to strange mandala could yet

have wings. What have I failed to see? Have I sagged,
the chauffeur's face smoking over the stretch limo hood
before the cathedral where the big man's daughter marries

to the hymn of Pachelbel? Have I been spent debris strewn
along the Mississippi levee riprap—sifted, lifted, broken to
indistinguishable scum? Cast-off condom fat with cream?

If I can dream, what can I do? Gleam in Robin's eyes, poster
of the slain not gone, you see? I didn't know I could
apprehend my brother in the Ursulines graffito *Keep*

Singing. I didn't know I could count my losses writ X-2-Zero
on the Ramparts door. I didn't know I could recall my mother's
tinsel hope in the crazy calliope played on the Natchez

but heard on Royal. I didn't know my room, 419 hotel le Richelieu,
could be suspended breathless historical over tears of sisters, blood
of the rebel, miser's nonchalance, basket makers, macaroni shops,

and circus grounds. I didn't know black rainbow shades of pain could
layer my skin. I didn't know there would be no peace until the end.
How could I know when I was nineteen, hungered to despair on that quay

in Marseilles, threadbare soul, heart torn, it would take some
forty years to find this fleur-de-lis on my Guinness head that Camber
drew at Molly's window on Decatur at dusk?

THE RIGHT TO BE FORGOTTEN

Among the many forms of wealth,
in the catalog of luxuries, I choose
the right to be forgotten on a quiet
morning such as this, to be this
foxglove footed among stones
beside the rivulet without a name
that steps deliberately down
from rain toward the rumor
of the sea. Rare privilege this
fame of the butterfly, wings
like flames, all flit and scamper
by whim of the spiral tongue
seeking what is sweet and free.

GREAT OLD MAN

Why fight it? Make it the goal.
Show the young folks how it's done.
I shall be the stalwart stumbler,
festive curmudgeon, codger
with canoodle, old coot
with bragging rights for verve
hard-won through physical attrition
but blazing in soul. No
begging bowl for me!
From the black hole where
my years went, a star shoots
brash and full—brief but
incandescent.

2

THE TORTURER'S WIFE

ALLEGIANCE

I pledge allegiance to the doomed life, clumsy
person, old salmon battering up a shallow stream.
Marked for hurt by this failing, arrested by a simple
glimpse of struggle or cruelty, I see the hopeful swagger
of a grown person in a child's bravado, or the childish hurt
in an old-face defeated stare. The weak syllable in a voice,
hitch of silence, hint of lessons taught by loss—
these plead my devotion.

Once I had a sweetgrass bag, but gave it away to a stranger.
"You have a sorrow," she said. "Don't be afraid to see
how deep it goes."

PEACE WARRIOR
for Kuku from Nigeria
singing in front of the bookstore

To be most brave, kill no one.
Be so still, others are called
from strife to listen. *Is that*
a song, under the shouting?

The language does not matter.
The only patriotism is devotion
to the garden of children. *Guard*
this place with gentle words.

Remember: this is the world
our mothers gave with
deep trust. *I bought this*
for you with pain.

THE TORTURER'S WIFE

When he comes to me at evening
for a time he sits still. This
I can understand. He looks through
my head, as if for someone else.

Then, for a time, he speaks
of ordinary things. I have learned
he is not yet here, with me.
He needs this emptiness.

When he touches me, the pain
from his hands enters my body,
a missile from the sky scorching
earth in the place I was born.

At evening, he does not speak of her,
my other—but in his eyes I see.
Breaking her has broken him.
Hurting her, how could he love?

CHAMPION THE ENEMY'S NEED

Ask about your enemy's wounds and scars.
Seek his hidden cause of trouble.
Feed your enemy's children.
Learn their word for *home*.

Repair their well.
Learn their sorrow's history.
Trace their lineage of the good.
Ask them for a song.

Make tea. Break bread.

HOW THEY RECRUIT CHILD SOLDIERS

Kill your father now with the hoe
at his feet! Then your mother!

If you ever return here—shame!
There will be no home for you
                          but with me.

If you run from me, I kill you.
If you fight for me, I feed you.

If you do not kill your father now,
then your mother—Do not look at her!

Look only at me! Do you see this gun!
If you do not kill your father now,

then your mother, you will lie beside them.
No one will tell this.

I give you one moment.

CITIZEN OF DARK TIMES

Agenda in a time of fear: Be not afraid.
When things go wrong, do right.
Set out by the half-light of the seeker.
For the well-lit problem begins to heal.

Learn tropism toward the difficult.
We have not arrived to explain, but to sing.
Young idealism ripens into an ethical life.
Prune back regret to let faith grow.

When you hit rock bottom, dig farther down.
Grief is the seed of singing, shame the seed of song.
Keep seeing what you are not saying.
Plunder your reticence.

Songbird guards a twig, its only weapon a song.

Who Knows about War?

If you weren't there, you don't know,
okay? If you didn't get shot at, you
can't talk about it. If you haven't seen

your sergeant lose it, it can't be real for you.
If you haven't lost your buddy—Bam!—keep
still, will you? Just keep out of it. If you

haven't fired in the thick of it, squeezed off
rounds through smoke and screams, and killed,
you don't get it. Won't get it. If you haven't hit

kids in a crossfire—those two got crazy,
ran the wrong way. If you never tried, after,
to tell a girl, in translation, who lost everything,

was found wandering the streets at dawn . . .
If you haven't lived years with a son who can't
laugh, can't cope, screams at night,

you don't know. If you haven't watched
TV generals with the sound off after
your brother is gone . . . If you haven't

ever managed to declare war personally
on people you have not met, how can you
say you know the first thing about war?

BENAZIR

The flower of our generation is cut.
What happens at the root?

The poorest have no begging bowl—
open hands, open eyes are the root.

Fury never wins—it changes us.
The flavor of losing is the root.

Who will wear the *dupatta* now?
Who will put down the gun at the root?

Is a bullet stronger than a word?
Who will speak for the root?

Many hands carry the pine coffin.
After burial, what happens at the root?

Our beloved sleeps beside her father.
She stood for him, after—her root.

The flower is cut in Rawalpindi.
Is the army safe—what is its root?

Can the strong man rule?
What can be his root?

A martyr rises through the sun roof.
Where does her power go from the root?

The shouting does not touch her now.
Open hands, open eyes, we are the root.

Torture Test

You have long experience. We favor you. You demonstrate
an intelligent turn of mind. All this is very good. But still
we need to ask if torture is right, what constitutes torture.

Waterboarding is repugnant, you say, to you, personally—but is
not torture, technically. Not torture, exactly, you say. I'm afraid
I don't understand your position. Perhaps with an experienced

witness we could settle this matter. Through the door at the far
end of this room you will see a table with restraints, and
a cloth to drape over someone's face, and water to pour—

and we will pour it slowly—over the cloth to simulate—
but only simulate, you understand—the experience
of drowning. The only question, your honor, is who

should we trust to experience this simulation, and tell us
how it is to think—but only to think, you understand—
that drowning is imminent—to gasp for air, for life,

for freedom. Should this be a senator, do you believe?
Should this be you? Your child? Your grandchild?
On this proud day, your family is in this room.

Please tell us who should lie down on the table now.

Suicide Bomber, Algiers

He saved his wages, went to Mecca twice.
He finished high school in prison.
Once out, he tried to sell ice cream.

His family home had no roof.
His empty bed became his mother's shrine.
His father remembered him as a good boy.

Prison was a school for losing hope.
The saddest person among us,
his uncle said, *is our greatest danger.*

How do we help that one,
for sorrow speaks in fire?
He disappeared for a year.

Maybe he went to the mountains.
Dawn there is the hardest time. Then
sorrow spoke in fire, explosion, death.

They handed the father his driver's license:
a smudge, the charred photo of the boy.

PICTISH STONES

History is silent on the meaning of these.
—sign at The Royal Museum of Scotland

Depicted horse, rider, death by ax
in blood-red sandstone, level zero
below the Kingdom of the Scots.
I put my hand where the sign says don't—
to apprehend the carver's chisel-work,
dizzied by the smoky bond between
sweet freedom and rusted violence
that goes back beyond the bitter
chronology of killing storied here.

History is silent. I must not be.

A Prayer by the Tigris

19 March 2003

Let me be light from the morning star,
the glimmer between worlds.
I am what you cannot see—at midnight
or noon. I am the child in war
putting my candle in a paper boat
at the call to prayer. My mother says
when I die I will be a secret.

Little boat, you are my sister
I put light in. Go find me
a place to be. Allah is great,
you are small. Go tell them
your brother is here. My mother,
my father, we—we are a secret,
we are a boat, we are a light.

We are the star that sees you.
What we lost will be you,
my mother says.

Green Zone, Green Earth

—after Du Fu

Going home along back roads, smoke from somewhere
I can't see, meeting those wounded by want, weeping,
youngest crying loudest. When I remembered Falujah,
where banners were smoke at dawn climbing to the rooftop
and beyond, where a horse could step into the sky. Below,
across the rutted ground, mines might break us
or the innocent.

Little flowers edge the torn road beside stone walls
smashed by Bradleys—made my mind reach around
the world to where simple things may yet be.
Blackberries, jewels of dew hidden in the ditch
back home, purple on your fingers, black as dusk
comes on, and then sweet summer rain—not this
road where ghosts walk home.

Beyond the hills, we came down at last, around tight
turns to the river. I left the others far behind. The mice,
guarding their grain, stood to listen for terror owls
like men at Basra before the fight. The moon feeds
on sticks and bones. Remember the troops positioned
to hold the bridge? How many stood, after, walked
for home? The human, the tender ones
did not stand up.

I, too, drowned in dust. Back now, back in America,
my hair whitened by the fury, to the mobile home, wife,
dressed at the Goodwill, sees me, cries the rain of
all our nights apart, rivers underground that surge.
My daughter, magic survivor, her face a ghost
of the good, turns away, afraid. Her shoes
leave a print as she scampers. Through
the screen, my son, his hand raised
against all this shouting, runs
to be folded in my arms.

I am not who left. Let me rest. Sleep.
There will be time, but look in my satchel
for something I brought you home. Dress uniform
wrapped around rose water, tiny bottle, the only
tender thing I could find in the rush to leave
the city of Baghdad.

They whisper questions, sniff the gift, look
at me shyly, cry out—wife, children, the place
itself. Who could ask them to be still?
What I left back there—and here,
the thunder of their words.

Elementary Lesson

Miss Miller, gentle wisp, my teacher
in grade four told us one afternoon
about the Fertile Crescent, the map's
green place between blue threads,
Tigris and Euphrates—the cradle,
she said, of civilization, and my
love for her became affection
for lavish words like Mesopotamia,
Hanging Gardens of Babylon,
Eden, Arabian Nights, and Ur.

If we don't get the story right,
she said, *Scheherazade will die.*

In war, the maps don't show this.
How can we get the story right,
one more chance to get it right
in Green Zone, Shock and Awe,
Depleted Uranium half-life doom
of a thousand and one nights of war?

Miss Miller, tell them what you
told us then: *Between the waters,*
people learned to get along.
Alphabets and grain and stories
were the money of those days.
Children, find in your big hearts
that place where we began.

Mrs. Smith, 1959

Her name, the way she stood, her station
in the larger world may not have been known,
but to me, to us, then, fifth grade, Cold War,
she was our calm. One trance-like afternoon
she read to us from a little book of terrors: John
Hershey, *Hiroshima*. Could this be happening:
a child with skin falling away, a mother clawing
through rubble we saw, were blinded by death
and our nation's act, in her voice without judgment
but deep sorrow? When Mrs. Smith looked over the top
of the book at us, we were a silence, waiting. *This
is about*, she said, *what we must never do again.*

How many heroes does one life need? For me,
that one. She gave lessons no one else in all
my years of schooling touched. By the time
she closed the book, I had become a child
neither television nor president nor any
strident voice could dissuade from
loyalty to the human way those
children walked among ruins
in the war-torn world.

NIGHT FLOWER MARKET ALONG THE WATER

Ho Chi Minh City is crazy tonight—everyone outside
shocked by the survival of human joy forty years
after the Tet Offensive. Tell about the eyes painted
on every boat to see a way through trouble. Tell
of homeless children on boats waving, of rice hulls
burned to make bricks, the one who named his plot
in the Mekong Delta *Peace Island* though he was
a soldier, a local hero scarred by Agent Orange.
He makes a meal for his visitors from America.

The night flower market along the water
was a dream that survived all those years
of war. Now, young strangers walk among
the grandchildren of their grandfathers' foes.
The night flower market shimmers in the water,
as love shimmered, was ghost, memory,
not real when one ran naked, screaming, and
another held a pistol to a neighbor's head,
or a bamboo stake, and the beautiful hand
of a child was trained to kill, and young men
far from home were trained to kill the child.
After the war, seeds of the human ache forth.

A monk will ask what you seek.
Three women weave a room-sized mat.
A girl will gaze as the boat passes.

What is inside our silence
as we gaze and wonder
at the beauty we bombed, not knowing
that after forty years this night would greet us
with the flower market along the water,
both sides lucky together in the world?

ESCALATION OF THE POSSIBLE

A child who shouts must feel powerless without shouting.
A man who picks up a gun must feel powerless without a gun.
A nation that drops bombs must feel powerless without them.
But what is power? What is a nation? What is a man?

A man is a child with greater responsibilities.
A nation is big enough to not need to be afraid.
A gun is an intricate invention of the powerless.
A woman poet shot shall have power over all.

Her words are suddenly our words.
What she can't say we must say.
Give good words to the child, give good
power to the man, give the nation forgiveness—

even if we can't solve all the problems right away.
It's when we hurry that we kill.
It's when we are afraid that we ripen a child
for shouting, needing a gun, wanting a bomb.

So we are growing another kind of world:
wise children learning to say at every meeting,
How is it with you? Where do you live?
What do you love? Please, you will show me?

We Ask the Iraqi Artists What It Is Like to Be Creators Where Civilization Began

The smudge of war falls from their eyes.
They become tall, grand humans.
We see each other at last.

We invented writing, says one.
And the wheel, says another.
We created the sewing.

Our rivers made paradise.
The light of the day shines
over us, it is time to gather

for a meal together, we need
to ask about each other's
families, and how to begin

a new era of life together.
And soon we are all chattering
like beautiful children

far from our foolishness.

Nadezhda

I have only visited by opening the paper,
but *Nadezhda*, Russian for 'hope,' code-
name for the barren lands in Kazakhstan
where Stalin's people tested nukes in '49,
year of my birth, has me by the heart—
soil puckered to glass, thick Geiger static
my century's dirge, birds wheeling,
and the cows, sheep, horses of the poor
grazing on wind-tousled grass.

Nadezhda had no post office
so spies might be fooled after *Joe
One*, our code for the first blast
tethered on a tower there, went
sky high and spattered concrete
bunkers with melted earth.

Nadezhda, Enola Gay, Big Boy,
Hiroshima—what shall we do
with these lyric nicknames for our
darkness? I close the news.

Nadezhda.

Proclamation for Peace

Whereas the world is a house on fire;
Whereas the nations are filled with shouting;
Whereas hope seems small, sometimes
    a single bird on a wire
    left by migration behind.

Whereas kindness is seldom in the news
    and peace an abstraction
    while war is real;

Whereas words are all I have;
Whereas my life is short;
Whereas I am afraid;
Whereas I am free—despite all
    fire and anger and fear;

Be it therefore resolved a song
    shall be my calling—a song
    not yet made shall be vocation
    and peaceful words the work
    of my remaining days.

BESIDE THE ROAD
WHILE OUR NATION IS AT WAR

In our son's young hand,
  borrowed from the ground in California,
  five acorns glisten and roll.
  "Dad! These could be bullets!
  Will you help me make a gun?"

His eyes look up into mine.

"Or Dad! They could be magic
  seeds! Will you help me
  make a bag with a hole—
  so they drop along the path
  and grow?" I take his hand in mine.

"Little friend, we must decide."

At the Indian Cemetery on the Oregon Coast

Take that path at the bend in the road (easy to miss)
and then up through salmonberry and salal

to where they had to chop away a long
spruce root to fit a few graves. You find only

the soldiers marked with stones: marble for James,
World War I, granite for Leonard, World War II,

then Raymond and Agnes, married in '45—
plastic roses, drenched flags in moss.

From there, a dozen wooden crosses, crooked
aluminum letters still: here lies NG, here W.

Someone made a bench of cedar planks nailed
to a cedar tree so the old ones could rest

after they cleared the fallen alder branches,
stamped flat the tracks of elk and deer.

Sit there. Time turns over. Remember
when they said it would be alright,

that peace would come, and we would be
so happy we wouldn't need to speak of it?

Look how Leo's cup has filled with rain.

3

LOST LEAVES OF EARTH

A Few Treasured Steps at Glensallagh

The cities are burning. The roads are
risky with haste. Life, some say, is short.
So here, the traveler can rest. Here, the fig tree
thrives against the wall, and all good things

are gathered in one abundance.
Arriving here, all roads have spent their use—
highway become a lane, lane a bosky track
crawling through shadows. The vehicle sleeps here,

single museum exhibit from a distant way of life.
This is the haven for a few treasured steps
from doorway to garden, from morning to evening.
Here, savor a snatch of song, in time with puttering task

the hands find their own way to, hum to the chore,
or settle on a warm stone and let the birds do the singing
where they, like you, have hidden their happiness in the
hazel thicket, under the old ash, rising with mist from the

mown field, or at the table late, the rim of lamplight.
Here, the old larch boards on the floor of the loft,
peppered with nail holes from their former life,
where you go for sleep, glitter like starlight underfoot.

ABE & I

FOUR SCORE AND SEVEN YEARS FROM NOW
our descendants will inherit on this continent
an older earth conceived in diversity and dedicated
to the recognition that all creatures live as one.
Now we are engaged in a great struggle, testing
whether this creation so conceived and so dedicated
can long endure. We are met in a great community
for that struggle. We have come to dedicate a portion
of our grief as a final resting-place for those creatures
who gave their lives departing from this creation.
It is fitting and proper that we should do this. In a
larger sense, we cannot dedicate, we cannot consecrate,
we cannot hallow this creation. The desperate creatures,
neglected children, vibrant cultures and local ways of being,
living and dead, who struggled here have consecrated it
far above our poor power to add or detract. The whole earth
will little note nor long remember what we say here,
but it can never forget what we now choose to do.
It is for us the living rather to be dedicated
to the unfinished work which they who struggled
and lost here have thus far so painfully clarified.
It is rather for us to be here dedicated to the great task
remaining before us—that from these tattered beauties
we take increased devotion to that cause for which
they lost their last full measure of living witness and of song—
that we here highly resolve that these dead shall not be joined
by an endless parade of others long in splendor, suddenly gone,

that this whole earth shall have a new birth in welcome to its own,
and that reconciliation of all creatures, by all creatures, and
for all creatures shall not perish from the earth.

In My Name

Insane chainsaws snarl through ancient trees—for me.
Gulf rigs suck crude below Caribbean coral—for me.
If a little spills—a slick, a toxic tide—it is for my comfort.

A child kneels on concrete to make shoes—for my feet.
Distant strangers whimper words I don't know, grovel,
scheme by moonlight, cross night borders, beg.

Mountains move to expose my coal in China.
Rivers run red to dye my shirt in India.
Armies fire on faces in my name in distant lands.

Fingers twitch triggers in oil countries—for my car to go.
Leaders lie, elections shout *freedom, patriot, economy*—
so I may hide. Stocks maim—for my golden years.

I touch the thermostat, open the fridge, turn my Volvo
key, tap my Mac space bar for email—and the Pacific
surges over Fiji, the Ogallala aquifer sinks away,

the Sahara's green rim withers, Greenland glaciers
calve and crumble, Peruvian children thirst, fiery
trees explode in Greece, Brazil, and Malibu.

I savor my bath heated by salmon-killing Columbia dams.
I crumble feta airlifted from Naxos. I sip Australian wine
jet smoke softened ice under the polar cub to bring me.

Many practice war on earth in my name. Don't
all earth citizens, hostage to my comfort, call
for a life more simple than I have ever known?

Earth Verse

1. Rise from Earth

red earth bears us
hidden seed eye blinks
water bead wicks damp
myriad grasses grapple light
birds hymn this swale
trout thrill rain pool
leaves savor dappled light
joy teases human lips
old *tamánawis* makes bounty
earth smoke softens dawn
wise voices settle strife
first father cherishes mother
then mother cherishes child
child reaches for sun
all are woven kin
fir cone clenches life
at red earth hill
shall we be home

2. Go to Earth

red earth holds us
old leaves furl fall
fire consumes dry wood
rain veil glistens down
frost binds living waters
root kink seeks cleft
storms make stone clay
rivers feed deep earth
springs on hillsides brim
trees kneel apples slump
troubles enter red earth
seeds hide to think
we find praise songs
kind hearts forgive all
tierra nos hace vivir
fir cone spends seed
at red earth hill
shall we be home

A Buddhist in Cattle Country

We heard a rumor she was on her way
to spend time in a quiet place alone
and met her first at the barbeque
out to the Z Ranch where

you had to see it through
her eyes: smoking carcasses
on spits turned slowly
over mesquite coals.

God, that meat was good!
Burl knows how to fix it right.
You had to give her credit,
too: she sipped a beer

and asked how cold it got
hereabouts, and where
could you go for books,
and was the sky always

amazing and gold like that?

Walking in an Old Forest with Our Young Son on My Back, I See the Fates of My Friends in Every Tree

Little one, do you see how this thin tree grows in the shade
of its father? Don't do that. Do you see how this trunk
turns around, always looking over its shoulder at the others?

That's hard. Do you see this old woman hollowed by fire?
Do you see how this one bent low when young, then tried
to rise? Do you see these two weaving their branches as one?

Do you see this one lightning shattered who yearned an ending
into his mind? Do you see these four growing in a row, where an
old one fell? And this one, old enough for a lichen coat?

Little one, put your hand on this trunk green
in a lucky place of tall sun. Oh my little friend.

CALLIGRAPHY OF STICKS

In the forest at evening I begin to see
how each stick on earth is a fallen soul—
once green on high, then shaded

as life ebbed, withering pale, growing
dry, letting go, and there they lie, side by side,
or crossing over one another, splayed, teaching me

the history of puzzle, riddle, rune. I bow in dim light
to decipher old gestures of yearning and surrender—
read our common tongue of curve, zigzag, kink.

Was it a wise child in the land of old first set
sticks together to become a character, a thought,
a word? Now, beside the lake at evening,

I find them as if washed up from another
realm, from our beginning, spelling out
our hopes and terrors, as one stick tapped

the shoulder of another when they were
tall in glory, living in the sky.

At the Meriwether Lewis Grave
on the Natchez Trace in Tennessee

Your epic journey came to this: a warm, still day, a flag
at half mast, and the stone plinth hewn to remember
your promise and your end that October night in 1809.

The Blackfoot tried to kill you, but only you had the skill
to get that done—caught in scandal, desperate to be good,
your final report to the president due too long ago.

A few stones from the hearth of the Grinder cabin
have been preserved to view, cicadas yammer
in the oak, tulip, and locust trees, and all

around your monument I find the field of palm-sized
blocks to mark the graves of pioneers Ollie, Frieda,
Rosa, Beulah, Harlan, Zada, Infant, and Unknown.

Your job for the president, he said: "to contribute
to the mass of information which it is interesting
for this administration to acquire."

How can a mass of facts inform a proper life?
How can your journal, the most profound rough
draft in American history, ever be complete?

The epic task remains: not to cross, but to understand
this land. Not to catalog but to integrate and sustain
this Eden. Not to discover, but to engage our people.

Buffalo, who first opened this trace through the mountains,
Choctaw and Chickasaw people made to trade its use away,
help us. Farther on along the Trace, soybean rows begin to yellow

and the brown stalks of field corn to rattle dry.

Listening in the Mountains
North from Santa Cruz

High on the ridge above Big Basin, I met Coyote stepping briskly
along the road—eyes bright, tail straight, looking not left nor right—
and it came to me that somewhere higher on a bald stone knob,
lolling in the sun, the spirits of the generations were yet stitching with
the soft basket of the woman and the blunt needle of the man
one people to the next all along the river of their being.

We are called to listen like Coyote far across dark hills
for the whimper and tender wail of our own kind, and then to seek
through thicket and gully, to meet, to play, to mate, to make cubs,
to teach those cubs to mark the secret path. We are called to read
the fine print in dust left by beetle and centipede,

to trace the scent thread of instinct that tells us
where we need to go. So I went down the road into the trees
and found by visceral luck campsite 170—that fallen redwood
hulk, that castle stump and hollow place to hide, that fire ring
with glistening charcoal where in the spring of 1957 late
at night, by firelight my father reached his hand

toward the ridge and said, "Is that Coyote? Listen."

The Bardo
at a Crack in the World

Some deep urge at the fault line raised the range
and somewhere high at a cleft in stone, gravity spoke water
for creatures gathered to sip salvation—elk, deer, bobcat,
skunk, mouse, and the billion seeds.

Somewhere below, we gathered to dwell, to hear our train
wail, our clock chime, to see Eden thrive in a story of the bees'
hum-honey toil, and learn to say no, no, and no to cruelty,
greed, anger, and yes to the mysteries.

When my toil is done, when all Good Works and Bad Mistakes
have been struck clean from the spall of my soul, and I have
finished scratching on the door of God, put me in a cleft
somewhere high beyond the fault.

Roe Deer

As an ogre might see, a tall
god watching the body impossibly
small against the car's hurtling
prow, then spinning up and
away, turning, falling, sputtering,
spinning at the gutter,
pin legs working—as an ogre
might see, a tall god
witnessing frenzied fright
at this centripetal focus
where all cars stop
in their trance—as an
ogre might, a tall god
looking, our gaze
pushes the small hind
upright and away
into the dark wood.

CROW & THISTLE

There may be luck for those despised
by the mighty—you may be cherished
by the fierce and wise. Exhibit Crow:
verb-named strut and shout
in black leather feathers glistening
who knows too well *Hell Waits*
for Sinners, and so saves
a secret lyric heard only
by its young. See fond hesitation
disguised in swagger when
the lone crow steps back and bows
for thunder in the thistle glistening
swale wind scoops neat—
grass flat, wings clenched, and away.

PALOUSE

Earth Day snow settled on rusted car bodies
that held the north bank where the river turned
among the rolling hills at Potlatch. We pulled mullein
spears from velvet earth to be warriors. Yellow flame
of willow, sumac fire. Be deaf a moment, be blind.
These hills are women that roll and waver still.

Green is up beside the fallow field, blond
crew-cut stubble combed. Straight furrow here
would make no sense, where earth brimmed
fat from the plow. Dazzle of rain across the blue—
when my car got bogged in mud on Woody Slope,
Russ and his boy came to pull me out.

A golden braid brings sunlight into wheat seed—
wheat, lentil, pea vine twig pulling life from earth,
all gone deep as alfalfa root to wick the future.
Summer night, a distant farm light at a seam
in the hills boxing secret custom: Take your mandolin
along the old road and stop somewhere under stars.

What is gone made what you see.
What is forgotten formed what you know.
When the world ends, Smoholla said,
the drum will sound. Elderberry beads
the thicket blue: magpie tailfeather's
rainbow sheen.

TRAIL REGISTER
AT CASCADE HEAD

Botuful

Way cool

God I've missed this

4 deer & beautiful sunset

4 deer and 2 slugs

Rad, cool and tiring

Very buitiful.

So quite and beautiful

My friend died this weekend. This
   was my place to say good-by

I enjoyed the grooviness

Thank you

Last Wish

In the desert when I was a child
I found a seam in rock where moss grew,
a green thread wet, and bees came
over my shoulder to thrust their tongues
deep into the spirit.
                         In the desert
when I was a child I found a flag
of flowers hidden below the lava flow
where a rabbit and I savored dawn.

In the desert when I was a child
the moon smelled of juniper, and stars
were my own shivering, and deep
in its canyon a river came
from where I would have to go
sometime before I died.
                         Many pleasures—
civilization, love, family—but then,
old man hitchhiker, I would say
"Let me out here." "Here?" "Here."
I would go listening my way to silence—
weeping, unrepentant, a set of tracks, the wind.

SMOKE

Under the last of the stars at the lake's edge, among
dying pines spiraling stark against the sky, taking off
my clothes for a swim, I see dim at the dock's end a rolling
ball of smoke, dusky and alive turning inside out, tapered
then a hump, a rope, a knot, a lump in the soot smudge of mist,
and then it separates—otter and two kits nursing,
nipping, chirping, rolling off to slide under
the water skin and gone.

Last of my clothes in a heap I walk the planks
from human toward the feral and dive into the dark
forsaking all the claptrap of my tribe for this life of smoke—
fluid, unencumbered, prickled by fresh cold rolling we
are smoke only for a little while, we are breath boxed,
brief treasure free, we are a combustion of joy
turning inside out under stars kindled, living, spent,
spiraling into the waters deep.

Lucky 4 a.m.

Little bird who wakes me in the dark
be molecule in the bonded chain of the good.

Sip of water who refreshes
be rain pilgrim winking through centuries.

Glimpse of gold sun out the office window
who catches breath, be one click

in the clock of beauty, benefactor of dimes
in a world of paltry millions that take us

far from what we love.

RUBY TAKES A STONE

One red wink among the glittering millions
catches Ruby's eye when the wave slides back
and this slanted trove of beaded pebbles loom

from deep danger to surrender one to the dimple
of her fist. Like heron beak, her wanting
cannot miss what nourishes—crimson lithic pearl

the waves dandied, polished, perfected
smaller in size and winsome shine until it matched
her love and went to pocket—to be found again

when morning waned . . . and again in a drawer
when she was grown . . . and again in a basket
with feathers and bone when a wee one called her

Gram . . . and again . . . and again . . . and again.

4

MARRIAGE IN DOG YEARS

THE BERRY FIELDS, 1959

Sweet crush so big it filled your mouth,
one fat Oregon strawberry made hot
by mid-day sun, seeded with
yellow nuggets like cornmeal & honey

gushing down your body inside,
outside, all over your hands & shirt
as you picked in fury, afraid to face
the strawberry girls one row over,

beautiful and profane, shouting
words you never heard before: *Don't
flip me the bone, you slut, I never
done it with him once.* You fill

the hallock, bow low, let yourself
eat one more big one, parceling out
rewards with a skill that will become
your life's long departure from perfect joy.

WILMA'S WANDERINGS

*Following Katrina and Rita, two storms
who have caught our recent attention, Wilma's
wanderings remain to be seen.*
—Radio Report

What fool would catch that last flight to the Florida coast,
get a cut-rate room in a sturdy motel, hunker down to
ride it out—TV shrill until it snapped to snow, then black—
dry lips grim when the first shudder hit the cinder blocks,
then exhilaration, terror at crescendo, the final distribution of debris?
Who—but every vivid soul hurtling into adolescent vertigo:

Remember age twelve?—climbing off your bike at the newspaper
dropbox where the guys crouched around a scrap of color spread
open on the dirt—Janet Pilgrim, Miss Infinity, looking right at you—
the caption *proud of her prow* where your puritan body writhed your
heart ignited your gaze narrowed then lost focus in a blur—your soul
pure dizzy with one eye dancing savage as a spinning top
across the Gulf.

A List of Wonders from the Time of Small

A door opens, closes. A book opens, closes. Morning
makes light, and evening takes light away.

They want me to be able to tell time. The little hand
is older, smaller, has more authority. The big hand
is more like a child—busy, playful, quick.

"When can we go camping again?"
"Sometime."

School hall, room, desk, inside my desk.
There are stages of privacy. Inside my mind
and outside the building are connected.

The book closes, light softens, the bell rings,
and I am sixty-nine.

Before I Could Be Human

In fifth grade, my teacher told my parents,
Kim is a dreamer. So my father said, *Make him
pay attention.* But she said, *No, I think I'll
let him be. He will attend when he is ready.*

Nights I heard the train and wanted to be gone.
I longed to be spirit—going far, seeing
everything, unrestrained. If they would
ignore me, I could find out who I was.

I heard crows and wanted to be that irreverent,
chatty, curious, a little dangerous, expendable.
But human, I must be otherwise. Wordless in myself,
I haunted the weedy edges of places, conversations.

It still comes at dawn—tug to slip out the door
and wander. I thought everyone else knew some
social secret—how to laugh together, or speak
a few words to a welcoming face, eager to know.

WHY I WAS MEDIEVAL AS A CHILD

Window was *vind-auga*, if I remember Old Norse
right—the 'wind-eye' for smoke to spiral out and light
to finger in at some hollowed cranny high by thatch,
open slot to let the stave-house breathe by dim
fjord or Iceland croft, to let wind hum hail
through gales in the dark time, and bring spring
bees down through that hole to sip at mead or spoon.
Cow and goat in their stall below the bed-shelf kept
the baby warm above. By night the wind-eye
allowed a star to gleam down where you rested
under bearskin. *Aðun het maðer* . . . the story began.
You dozed, brew horn in hand.

But then some lowlander had this plan to move
the animals out to the barn, and burn sand flat
to make glass, and seal us all in with ourselves—
no wind, no smoke, no star.

Take me back to furry damp, smoke,
plank with bread, and the sky knowing
how to get in.

When Writing Became Easy

I was in love.
It was not easy to be in love.
There was no choice in the matter.
I was far away—perhaps she had gone
with another. There was no way to know
so I began to write what came into my mind—
there on that rutted country road in New Mexico.
Words, stars, the horse named *Sueños*, the old
man with his roofless lumber mill bartering
boards for bread. Everything spoke, and I was
nothing but listening.

At Home

—for Perrin

When I lie down with my beloved, you
in the canoe, letting the world turn us round
and shuttle our lives where the current will
by channel, eddy, slough, we need to be long and
easy with one another, while paddles stroke
the softest water because the rain makes
everything smooth, and the river, receiving
the rain, and receiving your feet, and receiving
my hands, travels with a purpose we can't see
because we are low in our good work here.

Maybe, now that we know this, now
that we understand how the river keeps us,
you can see how, at fifty, with a young child
who must live long and learn much from our search
and his own, bathing in every water touching his place,
and with all our puzzlements about the century
and confused by our people's ways, I will need
your forgiveness when we lie down, my wife by
starlight and I, and our canoe its own
destination trembling in the river.

LATE NIGHT LOVE LETTER, NEW ORLEANS
—for Perrin

If I could be the lime green flicker of fire in the neon
    shamrock at Molly's at the Market;
If I could be the crescent moon tattoo on the shoulder
    of the girl child on Decatur; if I could be the spoke-tire
    spinning on the black boy's head, as he tap dance smooth
    as a water cloud;
If I could be the mule's ear that hears, the Tarot eye that sees,
    the sweat drop that rolls, the red silk that slips away, do you
    think I would be the blown-up color Xerox passport photo
    of an angry man taped to the cop car dashboard
    cruising Canal?
If I could be the close escape in the last shouted syllable,
    My dog ain't in that fight!—do you think I would need
    to fight?
If I could be the word, why be the blow?
If I could be pain purified into the feather of a crow,
    the concrete footprint of a life long gone; if I could be
    the line on the palm they call Long Life, intersecting
    with The Good; if I could be the angel of the square
    with wings and powdered face, folded hands, and a look
    of knowledge earned by grief, do you think I would
    be otherwise?
No choice, destiny.
Would the oak tree bless me then? Could a sinner say,
    I don't believe?
If I could be the attar of red wine in a coffee cup; if you
    could be the lip that drank, the torn sleeve, and we
    that moonlight shadow of a hand that beckons, we

the sacred heart magnolia opens every fist, we
the night hawk's diving cry, do you think we would
ever need to say, *So long*?

MARRIAGE IN DOG YEARS

No, really—this is a love poem,
you fool. I mean, it takes me
seven years of loving you

to diminish one year of shame
in your childhood—pouring
into the knot of your being

all I have to blur the memory
mirror that hurts you.
I can see it in your eyes,

hear it in your silences.
I can't take it away. But look,
my friend. Look at me, not

that infinite hall of reflected
scenes. Look at your beautiful
self through me, not that

fiery glance aside in 1963.

AUGUST, 1997

Our son does not yet have a name.
When he sneezes, he sneezes twice.
He likes to be held high on the chest.
His left leg stretches farther toward the sky.

At dawn on the closed curtain he stares
at the shadow of a moving leaf.
And when he feeds at his mother's breast
a sound comes from his throat that might be

the word in any language for peace, or yearning,
a boat at night gently tugging at its mooring,
like all the birch leaves at once shivering,
like rain stepping across the clover.

Our friends and relatives call on the telephone,
or sit beside him as he sleeps, whispering,
"And what will you call him . . . when
will you decide . . . what will be his name?"

Our Son at One Year Old

At the close of this sacred day we
have the bright idea of taking
him in the rowboat out on the
lake to view the moon rising, but
a few strokes from the dock he
fights his way out of his life
jacket for all his mother, frenzied
in the stern, can do, and lunges
for the oars—not one big oar
with two little hands, but
both, the way daddy does, and
there we are splashing up a storm
as the moon glides up to look:
little boy alive in the big world.

MILK

My wife pulled the grocery bag out of the car and swore.
Milk dribbled from a corner, then the bag gave way.
Want to hose the milk off your car's rug? I said.
I'll do it tomorrow, she said.
I knew what was coming, but I didn't say more.

Not tonight, but sometime tomorrow, her car would
smell like my VW bug in 1967, on the drive from L.A.
all night to Eugene with milk soaked into the worn
upholstery—rank, deep, indelible. All you can do eventually
is sell the car. Some things you can't even learn from
someone who loves you.

When my beloved has a day off, she dances in the kitchen,
and I see her. I see the real Perrin. The one whose hair
at the base of her neck smells like a forest after rain. The one
who sees into me and sets me straight. The one whose car
will smell like milk tomorrow, and I will roll down the window
on my side and love her.

I'm in for the long ride, so spare me the details.
Some things don't matter, and some things do.

Every So Once in a While

When I am in charge, you will see deep
into what I want, and make me understand.
Even the one in charge must surrender then.

When you are in charge, you will know
what you want, and tell me directly.
Then we will make it happen.

Who's in charge, you ask, *of when I'll be
in charge?* You look at me with that sly glance.
Then you are, and I am, and we do.

Home Alchemy

Midsummer evening we build a little fire
in the tin tub we keep for this pleasure
beyond the porch-steps feeding the flame

our scraps of creation—stair-tread end,
broken birdhouse, desk-top cutoff—and
with a dowel once meant to be an arrow

so I could do archery with our boy
the way my father did with me,
we roast a sausage over the embers

of lost intention. The posts are up
around the yard, but there is no fence.
I've lost my job, and money is tight.

Something will work out—maybe tomorrow.
My wife and I settle in two mended chairs,
our boy between as dusk comes, and then

the watermelon, and the moon.

Aunt Mar Changes How We See

She had taken to having naps
most afternoons in the side parlor
while the TV flickered, muttered
brash fuss or hush of snow

as the long hours rounded into dusk,
so dear Mar, when we found her,
lay settled in the easy chair where her
soft light had stepped to the window,

slipped free through the cold clear panes,
passed lively into the buds of cottonwood,
her whispered "Yes, oh yes" to wind and stars,
her way with folding hands, learned young

by lasting through the thirties, by raising nine
alone, by dealing books to hungry eyes in school,
by feeding us from the stove named Detroit Jewel,
her winsome prayers at times both hard and good

gone deep to the loyal roots of hickory, her calm
to elm reaching over the long prairie road
that joins the there of her
to the here of us, until it all

turns inside out, and through the world
beyond all trouble to core affections, no matter
how far or strange, we now see our days
by the gentle gaze of Mar.

TEN YEARS AFTER THE LAST WORDS

Ten years after my father, as he helped my mother
clean the kitchen when the blender had exploded,
scattering lime pie filling everywhere, said,
Better get another spatula . . .
and then fell dead to the floor,
I am standing at the wall with the sheetrock trowel
buttered with finish mud to cover the dimples
of the nails, the panel seam snug against the stud,
and I ask my father in my mind, "Daddy,
have I done enough for you?"

His voice blooms in my mind:
Years ago. Years ago you did enough.

"How can I choose between your work and mine?"

Again, his voice, fine as dust:
Do the work that is most alive.
Some days it may be mine,
Most days it will be your own.
And finally you won't know the difference.

With one stroke I close the seam.

Kindling

See these twigs, these splinters
of pine? We start small,
for the match makes a whisper
of fire, flaring in your hand's
cup, then settles as you bring it
to the kindling moment.
This is my lesson, my son—
for life, for love, for vocation
now that fire is in your hands.

In a Trance I Figure It All Out

No more worry about what has not happened yet.
No more anguish about what I have not yet done.

And while I'm at it, let my love be spoken
in what I do and do not do. This is my resolve.

And remember, I did not promise to be someone capable
outside my own little arena of joy and trouble. I only ask that

on my deathbed, I be allowed to have my feet stick out,
because otherwise they get hot and I feel confined.

I'll need to ask them to dim the lights in the room
because the dark has always been my friend.

If it's okay with others, maybe they could lower their voices
so that silence, old companion, can flow into my body.

Maybe they could take away all the books, calendars, clocks,
food, and words of encouragement so breath can be my teacher.

And as breath wanes, if it's not too much trouble, maybe
I could remember that moment in the desert when I was

a child, the sun just coming across the land to find me.

In the Children

My father raised his hand in the sun.
When I was young, he touched my head.
I asked him how to find my way.
He only looked at me and said,
Farewell, farewell. We will meet in the children.
Far away from this day we will meet in the children.

A luggage tag from his last bus ride
Is all I have of my brother now.
In the dark when I cry his name
He comes to me somehow:
Farewell, farewell. We will meet in the children.
Far away from this day we will meet in the children.

They are gone, the many we loved
In the trees, in the grass, and in the wind.
When a bird speaks low at dawn
We hear our kinfolk sing:
Farewell, farewell. We will meet in the children.
Far away from this day we will meet in the children.

Beloved, look in my eyes today,
While our boy on the meadow will run.
When we're gone, they'll remember we said,
Our love is long, and just begun.
Farewell, farewell. We will meet in the children.
Far away from this day we will meet in the children.

My father raised his hand in the sun.
When I was young, he touched my head.
I asked him how to find my way.
He only looked at me and said,
Farewell, farewell. We will meet in the children.
Far away from this day we will meet in the children.

ABOUT THE AUTHOR:

Kim Stafford is the author of a dozen books of poetry and prose, including *Having Everything Right: Essays of Place* (Confluence/Penguin & Japanese translation from Editions Papyrus); *Early Morning: Remembering My Father, William Stafford* (Graywolf Press); *The Muses Among Us: Eloquent Listening and Other Pleasures of the Writer's Craft* (U. Georgia Press); *100 Tricks Every Boy Can Do: How My Brother Disappeared* (Trinity U.P.); *We Got Here Together* (Harcourt Brace); *A Thousand Friends of Rain: New & Selected Poems* (Carnegie-Mellon U.P.); and *A Gypsy's History of the World* (Copper Canyon Press).

Stafford is the founding director of the Northwest Writing Institute at Lewis & Clark College in Oregon, and he has taught writing as a visiting artist in many colleges and schools in the United States, as well as in Scotland, Italy, and Bhutan.

In 1987, he co-founded the Fishtrap Writers Gathering, which holds an annual summer conference in remote northeastern Oregon, and he teaches regularly at the Richard Hugo House and the Sitka Center for Art & Ecology. He has received two NEA Writing Fellowships, and an Oregon Governor's Arts Award for his service to the writing community. Since 1993, he has been the literary executor for the Estate of William Stafford, collaborating with writers and editors to publish ten books by and about William Stafford, including *Ask Me: 100 Essential Poems* (Graywolf Press, 2014).

Kim Stafford lives in Portland, Oregon, with his wife and children.